Shapes

Squares

by Sarah L. Schuette

Reading Consultant:

Elena Bodrova, Ph.D., Senior Consultant

Mid-continent Research for Education and Learning

an imprint of Capstone Press

Mankato, Minnesota

A+ Books are published by Capstone Press
P.O. Box 669, 151 Good Counsel Drive, Mankato, Minnesota 56002.
http://www.capstone-press.com

1 2 3 4 5 6 07 06 05 04 03 02

Library of Congress Cataloging-in-Publication Data
Schuette, Sarah L., 1976–
    Squares / by Sarah L. Schuette.
    p.cm—(Shapes)
    Summary: Simple text, photographs, and illustrations show squares in everyday objects.
    Includes bibliographical references and index.
    ISBN 0-7368-1463-9 (hardcover)
    I. Square—Juvenile literature. [1.Square.] I.Title.
QA482 .S382 2003
516'.15—dc21

2002000896

Created by the A+ Team

Sarah L. Schuette, editor; Heather Kindseth, art director and designer; Jason Knudson, designer and illustrator; Angi Gahler, illustrator; Gary Sundermeyer, photographer; Nancy White, photo stylist

Note to Parents, Teachers, and Librarians

The Shapes series uses color photographs and a nonfiction format to introduce children to the shapes around them. It is designed to be read aloud to a pre-reader or to be read independently by an early reader. The images help early readers and listeners understand the text and concepts discussed. The book encourages further learning by including the following: Table of Contents, Words to Know, Read More, Internet Sites, and Index. Early readers may need assistance using these features.

Table of Contents

Playing with Squares   4

What Squares Do   10

Squares at Home   14

More Squares   24

Play Marshmallow Squares   28

Words to Know   30

Read More   31

Internet Sites   31

Index   32

4

Squares are shapes with four sides all the same.

A board for chess or
checkers has 64 squares.
Each game piece sits on
a square. Players move the
pieces to different squares.

A board of squares can make a game.

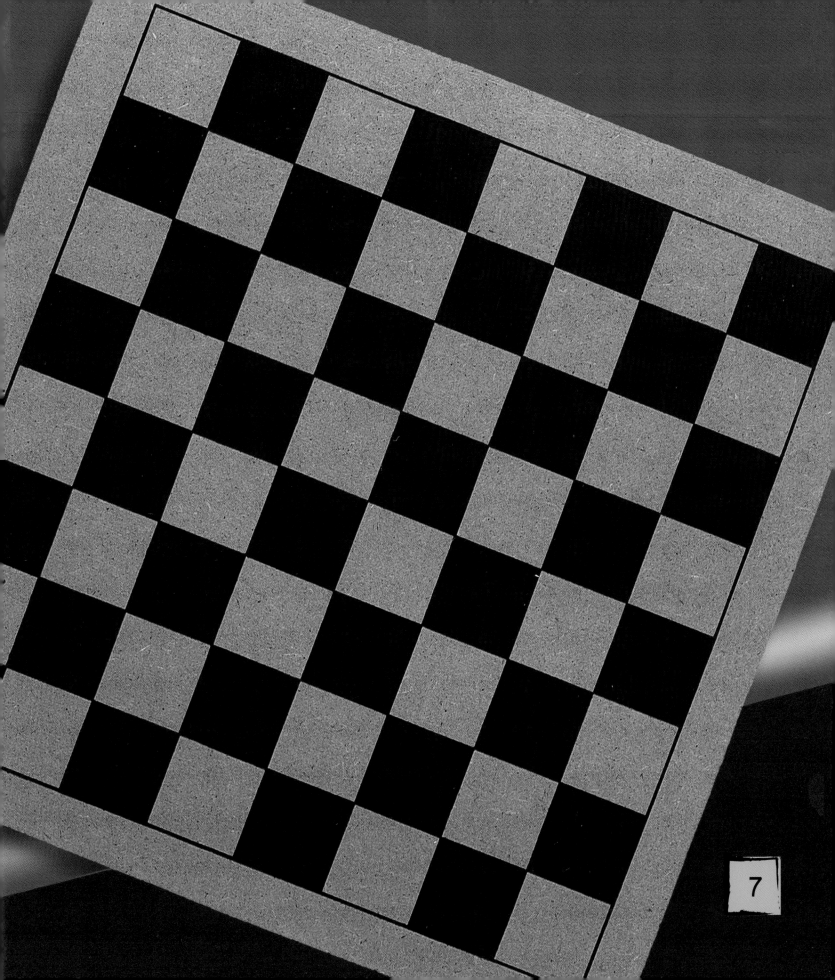

7

A sandbox square is where you play.

9

FEBRUARY

Sunday	Monday	Tuesday	Wednesday	Thursday	Friday
1	2	3	4	5	6
8	9	10	11	12	19
15	16	17	18	25	2
		23	24		

Saturday	
	7
13	14
20	21
27	28

Squares tell you the month and day.

A square can wrap
around your head.

14

A square can be a
slice of bread.

15

16

Quilters sew squares of cloth together to make a quilt. Quilts are warm covers on cold nights.

Slip under these squares and take a nap.

It is a good thing that we have napkins. Long ago, people wiped their dirty hands on their clothes.

At dinner you keep this square on your lap.

19

20

Some tables are covered with squares when we eat.

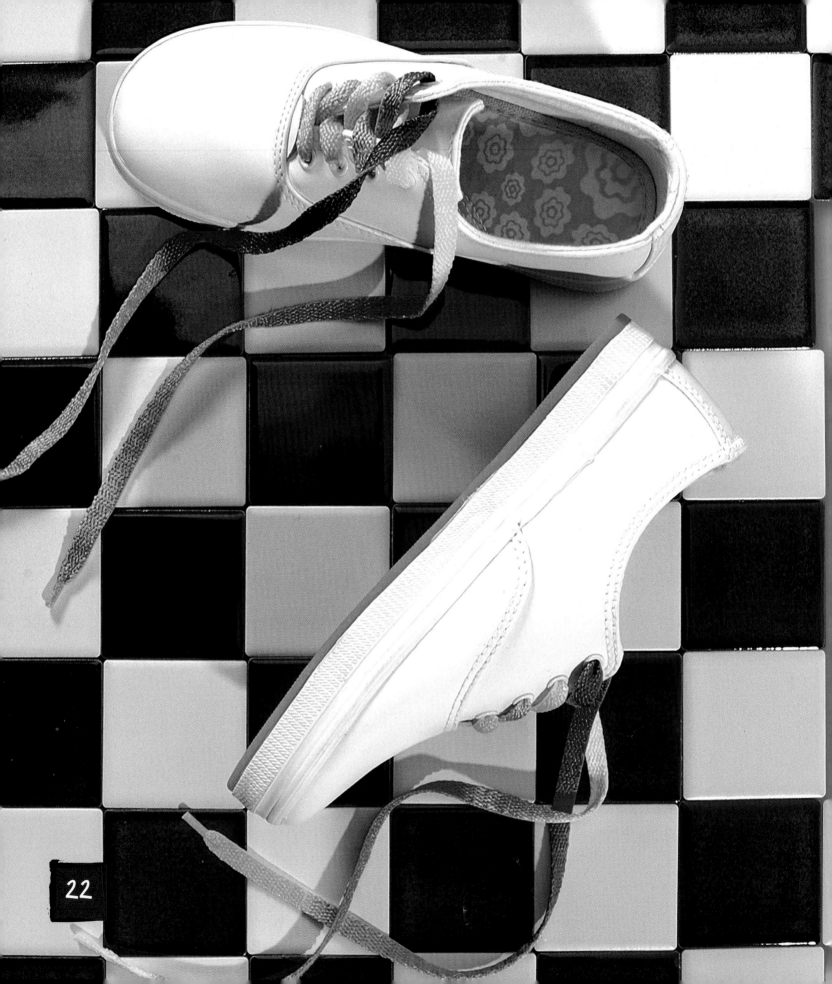

Square tiles decorate the floors of many homes. Some tiles are made out of clay. Clay tiles are baked in a kiln. A kiln is a very hot oven.

Small squares are floor tiles under your feet.

Sarah Square
123 Square Ave. S.
Squareville, S. D.
54321

A colorful square helps hold your letter.

Which of these shapes
do you know better?

Play Marshmallow Squares

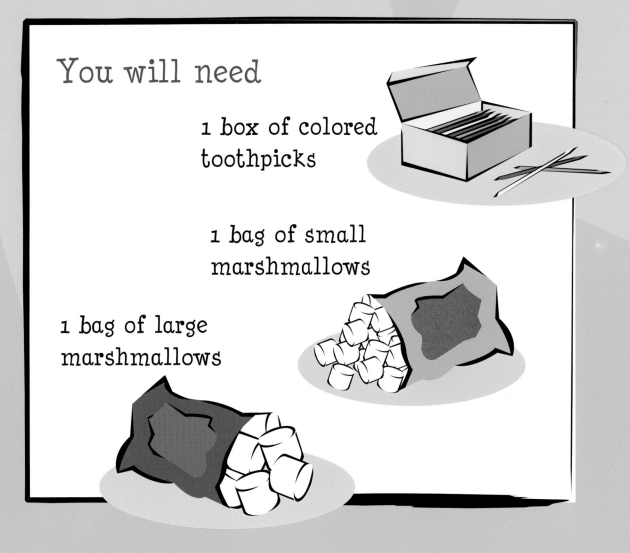

You will need

1 box of colored toothpicks

1 bag of small marshmallows

1 bag of large marshmallows

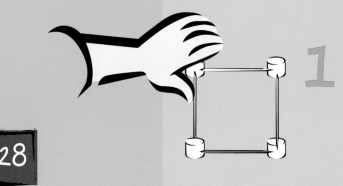

1 Connect four small marshmallows with four toothpicks to make a square.

2 Push another toothpick into one marshmallow in your square and build another square. Keep building until you have four squares across.

3 Now, build the squares going up until you have four rows of four.

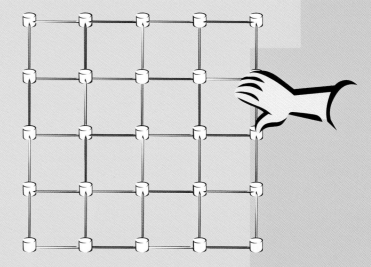

4 Place one large marshmallow into each square except one. Pick one marshmallow and jump over another marshmallow to land in the empty square. Remove the marshmallow that you jumped. You can skip around the board, picking different marshmallows to jump. Can you jump all of the marshmallows and only have one left on the board?

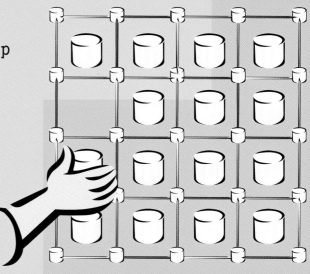

Words to Know

clay—a type of earth that can be shaped and baked to make bricks, pottery, and tile

decorate—to add things to a room or an object to make it look nice

kiln—a very hot oven that is used to bake objects made out of clay; the objects are baked until the clay is hard and dry.

napkin—a square piece of paper or cloth used to protect your clothing when you eat; you can use a napkin to wipe your hands and mouth during a meal.

quilt—a warm blanket; some quilts are made of square pieces of cloth called quilt blocks that are sewn together in a pattern.

tile—a square piece of stone, plastic, or baked clay; people put tiles on floors and walls; they can arrange the tiles to make pictures or patterns.